THE REFUGE OF TREES

LOOSE POETICS

JONATHAN SEILING

the refuge of trees:

loose poetics

Jonathan R. Seiling

Gelassenheit Publications
All artwork by Jonathan Seiling.

Ohni:kara 2020, revised October 2023.

ISBN: 978-0-9880993-1-9

CONTENTS

PSEUDO-SPIRITUAL

To Melissa,

Twenty years
of toes, tears and teas.

You're still telling me,
you don't like presents.

All you want
is a written note.

I hope this makes up
for the years
when notes were too short
or were left unwritten.

PSEUDO-SPIRITUAL

1.1 O, SPIRIT OF ROOTS AND BRANCHES

Moving forth in all directions,
growing life from seed and soil,
seeking every corner of the universe.

We find a place, connect to you
with sight, smell, touch, taste and hearing
in your wondrous life of eternal love
through your love for life eternally.

Your sun calls forth the budding leaves,
reaching skyward, bending
toward your seat
at the earth's core
within the clouds of unknowing.

Moisture of the earth
tugs

the tangled
roots

lower;

You draw us all into canopy,
encircling the trunk of your tree of life,
joining hands and singing praise to Creator;
meeting your natural world through senses,
your restoration of life,

a wherewithal of presence:

here, now, in a time and space,
where we belong within you
Cosmos within the creaturely,

a creation for the cosmic.

1.2 PINING FOR PEACE ON THIS LAND

(An Acknowledgement re:
Upper Canada Treaty
and
Anishinaabe, Ojibway, Haudenasaunee peoples)

It began at a time before I can recall,
that I was planted here as a seed,
having fallen upon a mess of matter:
moist earth filled with nutrients and minerals
for me to nestle
and be cradled in.

Who planted me here?
I have no idea,
but I know I'm part of an eternal circle
that can widen with each season,
which also shrinks
each time that mortar is mixed.

My seasons of coming and going,
of growth and decline;
these rhythms of birth and death,
of decay and transformation,
a process I share with all living beings around me:
they all shrink in horror
in the face of mixed mortar.

Mortar is the foundation of a new structure,
of the hardening – no!, of the permanent cementing
of the earth's crust.

Mortar spells death to the seasons and circles.
Square, flat, lifeless and listless,
whilst robbing all forms of their innate flexibility,
commanding cowardly fidelity.

As a pine tree,
I saw the busy mortar-people come and go,
wearing steel-toed boots as they worked.

I saw those who came before the mortar-people,
who often walked barefoot around me,
who stepped softly,
even when they would wear leather
to protect their feet.

I missed their soft steps,
while I saw armies of so many mortar-people
marching around with their designs,
plans for more and more cement.

Once, so many years ago,
though I remember like it was yesterday,

those who came before the mortar-people
had fought each other furiously,
perhaps hoping to rise up,
commanding all forces against the mortar-people,
in a way unlike living beings
who make a home in the forest,
and I pined for them to stop.

Finally, one day they met at my trunk,
using strong, sharpened branches
to dig a deep hole,
one which exposed my roots,
and left me almost panicked
as to what would come next.

And there, at my once hidden depth,
in the place I'm rooted
most intimately to earth,
far below,
in the quietude of the sub-mortar-world,
they buried their hatchet beneath my feet.

That was many years ago,
and ever since then,
my toes have found delight
twisting and matting
a web of tiny roots,
binding that hatchet to my inner core.

I'm still guarding it for those who came before,
who placed it within my tangled depth,
and here I pine for more peace.

Whenever I see mortar-people,
I want to tell them this story.
I want to expose my roots again,
in a naked protest against mortar,
crying out to them: "cement kills forest life!"

I want to show them the hatchet,
which both threatens my life,
and the grey matter
within the skulls of the mortar-people,
and the lives
of all those who came before.

1.3 Redefining a Wild Man

Will there be a day
when civility is scorned
as the unnatural disease it has become,
ever since the day we decided
to capture, contain, tame and train
the fire stolen from the gods?

Hey look!
There's a man
dressed in a way
that belies his weakness,
his pathetic civility,
in his ineptitude and unpreparedness
for the break to happen.
When all becomes broken,
what can this guy fix?
When his means of communication all fail,
no phone or apps to command,
no longer any services and servitudes of others,

can this guy even light a match,
fire up a bit of warmth,
make clean water,
cook a meal?

When everything hurts,
does he possess the wildness,
is he possessed by *wilder*ness;
is he just wily, already too wiled,
or can he finally become wilder,
and so thus able to find strength in the uncivil,
in being reborn as
bearing divinely vestigial bornedness,
natura naturata?

Or is his power sunken in the mighty dollar,
the digit,
the network,
the fictional stock?

How does the wild man
turn his back on civility,
except to turn his face
toward his cosmic Mother,
to bask in the gaze of insuperable nature?

1.4 VITAMIN N.N.

I arrived here countless moons ago,
    becoming rooted in a patch of soil,
    next to a strip mall.

I used to have dear friends
    and even relatives close by,
    but now I stand alone,
    amid the comings and goings
    of too many gas guzzlers.

Cough cough. ....
    /inhale\exhale.
    There we go, that's better.

At the edge of the mall,
    there once was a den of foxes,
    sheltered by a pile of sapless old members,
    a place no rabbit dared to venture;
    now there sits a mortar chunk,

nearly as tall as me.

Black crusted earth,
stinking of tar,
with light grey perma-formations surrounding,
keeping the gas guzzlers in line.

A green cross,
a lime plus sign,
marking the building
just over a branch length from my core.

It mystifies me.
I've never been inside.
But oh, the comings and goings,
it makes me blush verdant with envy.

The sick, the weary, the heartless, the hopeless,
they enter, they wait,
and they leave with a little white paper bag.
I guess it gives them hope.
Or heart.
Or spunk!
Or health?

Yet they keep coming back,
often returning as downtrodden,
as when they first came.

I like to play alongside,
Give them life, a lift.

I reach out my branches in summer,
with shade as they pass under my breadth

and move within my neath.

In fall, I fling my dead leaves at them,
sometimes even pinching their cheeks,
or tussling their hair about,
just to get a rise.

In winter, I'm a mimer,
with my bare limbs and branches,
muted dance with the light and shadows,
a pantomime of paradox.

Then in spring, when they've seen enough,
of the sarky and acerbic entertainment I offered,
I burst into leafy luxury again,
and I pump out my N.N.

I watch comings and goings,
many ignore me,
but some give me a smile,
and a few even stop,
with a cough cough. ....
/inhale\exhale.
There we go, that's better.

But inside every one of them,
I know they all know,
the green cross is fake pharma,
and me, with *natura naturata*,
I'm their redemptive saviour,
full of grace,
N.N. is with thee.
And so is hope, hearts, spunk and health!

1.5 THE BALLAD OF OLD MAN FRASER

(in gratitude to Emerson and Elsie McDowell and the whole Fraser Lake Camp family)

In the rich older days of a century ago
Lived a man who knew money and power galore
He had all that he wanted that money could buy
Till one day he just stopped, stood there and asked why?...and said

Hey hey hey (x2)
I don't belong in the world, I fear, not this version I know
I must head out of town, where else life could go

As a young man he'd go to the church on his street
He learned how to pray nice and when to get on his feet
So seldom he felt God's Spirit was there
He stopped going to church, stayed home and just stared and said

Hey hey hey (x2)
I don't belong in the church, I fear, not this version I know
I must head out of town, where God wants me to go

So he walked to Fort Stewart, sought the heart of this land
From Old Barn to Lone Pine he saw the work of God's hand
From the Tree House to Mosquito Point on he went
The stars up above made a heaven-shaped tent, he said

Hey hey hey (x2)
I'll belong here always
Yes, at this lake I'll pray, and make it my church
Throughout all my days days days
I'll belong here always

By this lake he'd sit and he found deeper peace
He breathed the rich air, felt the Spirit release
Then he called out and said to all folks that he met
"let's call this our church, God's green forest bed and..."

Hey hey hey (x2)
We'll belong here always
At this lake we'll pray, and make it our church
Throughout all our days days days
We'll belong here always

The folks came out from all over the place
Each gender, all leanings and every race,
Inviting all others whose spirits would soar,
Let's be here together and forever grow strong and then

Hey hey hey (x2)
We unite and belong
With trees and the soil
God planted us all
With spirits to roam

Slowly they walked and sat down at Lone Pine
Brought cares of their lives and got closer to fine
This camp here grew out of the love they'd all share
And they'd return with full hearts to their towns everywhere, saying

Hey hey hey (x2)
We belong anywhere, always
Wherever we stray
Throughout all our days days days
We'll belong in this world always

1.6 Northern Winter

The northern winter is my warmest comfort.

The sullen, grimly-reaped tree skeletons incline,
    Next to sassy coniferous dandies,
    Who brag as they come fully alive in the depth of a chill.

I'm thrown into gear by my metabolism,
    Battling the body's tendency toward the grave,
    Increasing my heart rate, honing my motivational focus.

I know of a warm fireplace,
    Where a dog lies peacefully at rest.
    Thoughts flooded with activities under the summer sun,
    Yet a subconscious knowledge, stings of the icy storm outside.

I dream of what is yet to come and love the northern winters.

1.7 Norm's Song

A place where you want to be
    is a wonderful feeling
    stuck inside on a rainy day
    still everything is ok

Wind flowing right through your hair
    loons floating on water there
    nothing buzzing beside my head
    nice and relaxed in my bed

            blue above, blue below, green through me

Hearing calls of loons and owls
    wait is that a wolf who howls?
    I'm up here on a balcony
    sipping my tasty mint tea

Dragonfly guarding our peace of mind
soon some firewood we must find
but how far will we need to hike
for the kind of wood we'd like?

1.8 Lone Pine Lullaby

The day is through
the sun is setting low
our hearts are full
and our pace is slow
we sing a lone pine lullaby
a little lone pine lullaby

We whistle a tune
it puts a smile on our lips
our eyes go closed
as we sway our hips
we feel a lone pine lullaby
a little lone pine lullaby

Our ears are awake
but our head's asleep
our thoughts go up
as we're resting deep
we hear a lone pine lullaby

a little lone pine lullaby

When we're back home
and we feel alone
we remember these days
this place, these friends
we shared a lone pine lullaby
a little lone pine lullaby

1.9 BRANCHES WILL SALVE THE WOUND

As one who has gained the title,

doctor philosophicus,

with the rusticorum of the Rus'

in the domain ruled

by the Queen of the sciences;

and having been completely baffled

at those dressed in rags,

who dig for their last rubles,

and choose to buy flowers over food,

may I be permitted

to parrot and to paraphrase

that noblest of novelists:

КРАСОТА СПАСЕТ МИР

Yes, pardon me for insisting like an idiot,

but branches will salve the wound.

1.10 TRANSPLANTED AND TWAIN

two trees transplanted
Together. Between.
Both trying to root in the soil
Both reaching upward to the sun
Both gazing outward, inward and across at the other

rooting, reaching, gazing

the run rises

shining first on the eastern.

the western sits in its shade
awakening slower

while eastern's sap gets flowing

now ready to continue
the slow, beautiful life of growth

communion with its partner

the sun now at full height
beats down on both
gifting flow of energy
through leaves

as the sun sets the eastern is first
to feel this loss, the darkness

with the western tree straining
to take in the last streams of light.

in the dark of night

eastern

and

western

end their
gazing, reaching, rooting

they turn inward to examine their core
resting twain their limbs
feeling their strength
as sap draws through their roots
up from their bed of soul.

again connecting as self-communing with their core
extending their oneness, their whole
into their rooted, gazing, reaching
friend nearby

I.II PLEASE PLEASE PLEASE, STOP

The world has got a problem and we'll soon be down
and out,
The trees are being raped, it's true there is no doubt,
It's time to end this crime, it's tearing us to pieces,
The animals and plants you know, and dying by the
species.

So please please please,
Stop choppin down them trees,
Please please please,
Cause we're beggin on our knees,
We're sitting with unease
While they're killing birds and bees,
And it stinks like rotten cheese
That they keep choppin down them trees.

Well we might have a solution to this thing we call
tree-rape,

And we don't need a Superman with a big red super
cape,
We need Tarzan, we need Jane, we need Abel and
we need Cain,
We need people who are nomads, cause develop-
ment's insane.

The first thing we must do for our scheme to work as
planned,
We must try to stop the chop, this'll be our first
demand,
Then we'll plant new trees in place via jobless
lumberjacks,
You ask us how we'll fund it, we'll make logging
firms pay tax.

Now surely your next question asks how new trees
could earn money,
The answers rather simple, though perhaps a little
funny,
They'll grow into a jungle, be a home for beast and
lark,
The tourists will come flocking just to see the new
tree park.

Another thing's MacDonald's burgs, and besides the
fact they're gross,
Beside the fact they taste much worse than month-
old raisin toast,
Everyone should boycott them, we could sanction
them with ease,
And the farmers who cut trees for beef, could take up
planting trees.

Now the last and final tree concern is to ensure that
folks will know,
Of how the trees are taken, and how they'll never
grow,
We need to educate the folks, tell them trees give air
to breath,
We only want to help them, we've nothing up our
sleeve.

Maybe these ideas seem a bit idealistic,
We know the Feds are stuck for cash, that we don't
deny,
But don't say it's impossible, we must give it a try,
The future's in the trees, so we can't be nihilistic.

1.12 We Recline and Mock Sorrow

What quiet gentle stillness she offers:
  an extended canopy of refuge;
  we face directly, awaiting silent exclamation:
  her focus encases swirling thoughts,
  drawing me deep into the unspoken conversation
  which tangles our souls,
  and makes thought leap from our eyes.

There is no leading.
Violence vanquished.

We recline,
  engaging the comfort of what holds
  us in the strength
  of the shared together.

We pacify each other,
  to bring out the rage which wallows within us,
  unbeknownst to our unmechanical consciousness.

= + = + =

Yet amid a world of suffering
the very thought of sorrow
is mocked in her gaze,
as though the well of joy
ebullient within her,
with only a thin layer of solemnity,
covers this boundless treasure:

The pearl,
given only to those
who can enter in truth,
and not in greed.

The gift given,
only to those
who can accept and respond,
who will show their joy
and model it for all to behold,
to give it to another
who has lost awareness.

1.13 FACE IN THE MIRROR

...
hebe ich vereinsamt
meine Hände zur Dir empor,
zu Dem ich fliehe,
...
ich will Dich kennen,
Unbekannter!

F. Nietzsche, *Dem Unbekannten Gott*

Sitting in the middle of a time,
resting a tired hand on the massive trunk,
a mirror appears within the bark.
A bee skirting behind my back,
dances on the stage
now lit by the sun-drenched arboreal backdrop.

A moment now bursting with Pandora's possibilities,
poised in the midst

of coming from
and going toward.

Catch a quiet glance in a mirror:
this countenance, this perhaps-being,
is not quite exactly yourself,
only the face shown to Libra,
expectant for affirmation.

Peering into the eyes,
Memories jogged about who this person is:
What she has done.
Whom she has loved.
Where she has been.

Faded glimpses at best,
the parting limbs draw
forth an embrace.

The face in the mirror poses the question:
Whereto? What next?

The space dividing the image from the mirror
allows for breathing room;
nothing to answer, all the questions poised
by the face apposing.

A demand to know – what's next? –
now set aside,
a step from the middle of that moment,
remembering the seconds, minutes, hours:
the eternity that brought us here.

Some were good moments and others could have been better,

all containing an element of what is floating around,
making thoughts wonder, who is this masquerading,
the facial προσωποποιία,
quidem persona, in the mirror?

Hoping that united they will now make some sense,
and guide the wandering *id* to understand,
entering into the mirror's glass.

United they only bring further yearning to go beyond,
to seek fullness in what lies ahead.

Memories leading into the hope of knowing what it all is,
and could become
when the next steps in time aim untoward.

1.14 TOMORROW'S FAMILY TREE: 2B

Ear to the ground,
nose to the stinking grindstone,
stiff upper lip, eyes on the road,
sensing it all like an electric shock.
Such rich intensity, emotive force;
of what becomes I know naught.
Yet it's as though awaiting
the rational culmination of what is sensed,
assuming the joy of some future's events
are hidden in the labour pains of today.

Beyond regret, abandonment, confusion, disorientation and relocation, I find a place 2B.

In my grandma's arms,
I fall asleep,
and dream about our progeny,
the family tree
with rings and limbs;

those unborn strangers
who someday remember us
+ think,=
how merry and simple
our lives must have been.

And if only I listen closely enough,
    and see clearly enough,
    and strain enough to become so sensing,
    as only to harness that emotive force,
    might the forward-leanings
    of today's cries of the soil,
    and aches of the soul,
    speak tomorrow's agenda,
    to one who cannot believe
    in a new day's dawn?

1.15 IF YOU'RE LOST, FIND A FOREST

As one who committed to study the divine science,
a wrestling-type relationship with God
for most of a lifetime
(starting around age 12 or so, I think?),
the moment of slumbered awakening,
at 14 years old,
the sure founding of God's finding.

Lost, intentionally so.
In a forest, sort of.
Probably a few metres in from the shore,
so not deep in the woods.
However, it was dark,
so that always counts as lost, right?
Nothing like darkness,
to reveal a hidden awareness.

No means to find a way around

or navigate to get further than the patch of earth
lain with a sleeping bag
and settling down for the night.

The earth covered with roots,
just enough for comfort to lay beyond reach,
while still hosting a somnolent, though awkward contortion,
back twisted upon the ground, laying
hopefully motionless until the sun came up.

I came by canoe,
and a serene night air
floated me there.

Securing the canoe to a root with a rope,
not knowing who would share this space and time with me
for the next several hours,
nothing to do but cocoon.

The bugs were horrible.
I think it was July.
They swarmed around my head,
so I pulled the opening shut on the mummy sac hood,
until I could peep out and still breathe.

And then the reality: breathing wasn't that important,
and getting used to the fragrance in the sleeping bag,
the result of a few unshowered days in Algonquin,
I task my lungs
with scouring that fabric encasement,
enough oxygen for a night's rest.

Then to close the opening
    so that only my eyes would peer out into the night sky,
    which was the most glorious I'd seen in ages.
    Now stamped onto my soul.

So there I was, a two-eyed sleeping bag:
    a self-contained lung would suffice
    for a few hours of restful breathing.
    Thus lost, but found.

Letting myself wander to a place I knew not,
    setting up camp on a spot where I could barely see,
    and unable to move,
    my only communication with the world
    my eyes,
    in wonder,
    soon to shut;
    my mind,
    gasping to catch up
    with the scene unfolding.

God and me there,
    finding God's foundation,
    lost in wonder.

Admitting I didn't know who I really was,
    what I should do with my life,
    but identity and purpose in that forest.
    Self-enclosed, still seeing and breathing,
    and wandering about an existence of wonder.
    Did I mention I was 14?

Beheld in the fingers of tree roots,

which were boney
and so far from a plush sofa.

To be still, to relax, to let go,
get even loster.
I had needed to find a forest.

1.16 POST-VESTIGIANA

My sight was open, set to spy,
for hints of evidence, which I,
in gazing at Beyond, up close,
hubristically, then soon I froze,
and blindness struck my retin-eye,

Now straining for the pitch of grace,
a metered dose, a vibral trace,
the echo in my core did buzz,
I cried for God to clear the fuzz,
*no chorus-*theos *to embrace.*

I searched for God within my heart
had wandered on, a day for naught,
my brain and sense I knew they could,
forbid the touch of mind with wood,
and thoughts from feels I saw depart.

Now to return unto my fold,

with empty hands, no-thing to hold,
of That which lay beyond my reach,
no tale to tell or truth to preach,
my barrenness, an empty mould.

As here I deign to know the All,
yet ken it naught, no-thing withal,
but only this, no vestigia,
a ruse or game, bellezza mia,
a broken heart, still wondering.

(a tribute to Bliss Carmen)

1.17 Hike Ooze

roots tack trunk to soil
saps push branch to atmosphere
leaves take sun to core

naturans quid est
green-brown the forms evolving
naturata sic!

1.18 THE ADVENTAGE

E
very one
talks about
how great summer is,
but I cozy up to winter,
and the Advent I experience,
when I get to stand out in my
glory.

Yes, part of
my heart sinks,
when the leaves of my
neighbours turn a glorious
yellow-orange-red-brown,
but I can't help feeling a sneaky
sort of excitement
at
their

loss,

in
my
pokey
leaflessness
coming into focus
and everyone wants
me!

Am I steady throughout the seasons?
Darn right, I am!
Am I also jealous how,
from spring through autumn,
as leafy neighbours become the object of games,
building projects, swings, homes for animals of all sorts?
But I know Advent will change everything!

I know that when leafy neighbours are denuded,
going dormant for a goodly long season,
that's when I get some longed-for attention.
And all sorts!

I'm the object of glorious decor,
strung with lights,
choruses strummed and sung at my twigtips,
even candles hang gently onto my finer branches.

Oh, how I glow and I glory and it lasts a jolly season long.
Folks bring me into their homes for this reason,
but first they chop me off at the ankles,
and then set me into a little pot,

where I get to drink water constantly.

Does this hurt?
Yeah, sure it does!
Is it worth it?
Um, yeah, I should think so!

I know I'm on life support for the next while,
but toward the end,
I'm surrounded by bunch of colourful boxes,
the object of much anticipation and joy.
*Such is merely a dis*advent*age at Christmas*
and I return to the soil that made me.

QUASI-SCRIPTURAL

2.1 LIKE A VIRUS

In the beginning
    you set out a tree for us,
    the One that could speak to our question:
    what is good and evil?

A wise or unwise serpent tricked us into eating the answer.
    I lost my dove-like innocence and loved the feeling.
    And we digested and metabolized
    that Answer.

The more we ate,
    the more we trusted it.
    We ate so much,
    it felt like the Answer was inside us to stay.
    We devoured it, addictively
    as though our existence depended on it.

. . .

Then, like a virus
infecting us with the power of self,
we could try to know what was good or evil,
and we didn't need the tree to tell us.
We. Could. Try.
We had bellies full of the Answer,
and we could just trust our rotting gut.

And now I'm trying to find a rock to sit upon,
where I can ponder good and evil,
while my stomach is empty.

The tree cut down.
The answers decayed.
No seeds survived.

I can't find a rock
comfy enough,
convenient enough,
or attractive enough to sit upon.
They all seem dirty, wet, bumpy, cold, gross.
So I wander the beach.

Shall I skip stones into your abyss,
having lost sight of the wisdom of trees?

Escaping to the jungle,
now becoming lost in your barren wilderness,
to the end.

2.2 WISDOM TREE OF LIFE

My *vita floricana*
has depths and heights and breadth,
beyond calculation or imagination.
It is, as a wise being is.
I take hold of this plant of life,
which was lain as a seed at the start of it all.
Before there was calculation or imagination,
there was a planting of a seed.

Ever after there will be growth,
even as there will be times of rot,
decaying branches,
even a trunk that becomes hollow,
and times when branches bend wearily
under the sway of forceful winds.

But they too produce seeds of wisdom,
as they sprout their shoots of leaves,
and shelter us in the heat of the sun.

2.3 VESTIGIBUS OMNIBUS

At pains to gain understanding from life's creatures,
    I have tried to plunder wisdom from the aged.

Just as my tongue grasps at flavours,
    my ears have strained to pick up the Word,
    vestigibus omnibus.

All I get are gasps of the Breath,
    as it's held gently within the palm of Charity,
    yet it was precisely from this cupped hand,
    that the bounty of all life sprang forth,
    and gushes ever further.

That much is clear *per vestigium*,
    as I was informed
    by those who dwell in the watery depths,
    by those who fly through the luminous heights,
    and in the Word spoken by all who move on the lands.

2.4 LOSING THE CO-CREATING SPARK

Everywhere we listen to the Name spoken in creation.
From birth it is our nature to sing to the One.

The tunes blare
above the drone of the nay-sayer,
overtop and above the haters.

I look up and your face is horizon-wide,
clouds and stars freckle your brow,
the moon and sun are like your watchful eyes over us.

We peer at our reflections. See how tiny we are?

And we ask, why do you bother with ants like us?

Had we listened to you and done our jobs,
tending your nature as you asked,
we would have remained by your side,
co-creating with your spark within us.

2.5 POLITICAL ROOTS

Oh, to have been a tree around Jerusalem!
    Or now, to be a tree around Washington DC,
    Moscow, Brussels, Beijing?
    Do they stay rigid,
    or balance and flex,
    even as they see imbalance everywhere,
    excepting the concrete jungle in which they stand
    like strangers
    who know not a word that is being spoken all around them,
    yet thirst for water, and communion,
    life-blood.

Yes, a tree hopes that if the roots are deep enough,
    even an axe will not sever it from its life system.

But if the very soil where it lives becomes utterly barren,
    dried out,
    diseased,
    toxic,

what can it do but beg
for birds to fly by and shit upon it?

Like stumps, feeling so depleted,
seeing more life and stock value
in the business of organic fertilizer,
than in the great halls of academia,
the stadiums of athletic champions,
and the palatial tech of the nouveau-riche.

2.6 War on Humans or Trees?

The impracticalities of war:
    trees and humans.
    Which matters more?

I'd be a monster to answer that question,
    and I'm loath to acknowledge the monster who even posed it!

If I'm at war with humans, indeed,
    if I've degraded my nature so basely,
    throwing myself at the mercy of violent instinct,
    gambling on the risk of winning or losing it all in battle,
    deigning that my life come bereft
    of breath beyond this contest,
    then what of the trees who are in my path,
    those who convert Co2 into Spirit?

To hell with them too?
    Am I now becoming a monster,
    in now answering this accursed question?

I have only so much energy for a day of battle.
    I need to regain my strength,
    seeking shade,
    nourishing fruit or nuts,
    perhaps even a place to hide.

Humans don't provide any of those things in battle.
    Not without the help of trees!
    Humans, those on my side and those opposing,
    they are all my enemy,
    with trees being my only true friends.

While I roll the dice
    on overcoming the Other,
    I'm locked into the stratagem,
    giving up my individual creativity and free will,
    as I submit myself to the nameless throng of forces,
    and the trees wave to me,
    bidding me to find refuge in them.

I shall not cut them down.
    I shall beat my axe into an apple-sauce strainer!
    Somehow.

2.7 POTATOES AND PEANUTS

Can I still bear fruit in a time of drought?

Are my roots deep enough,
    spread out with enough breadth,
    that they, still, draw on vestiges of moisture,
    even when the earth's crust appears parched?

I hate the heat when it comes and doesn't relent.
    Then I want to become all roots.

But roots can't bear fruit,
    unless you're
    full of potatoes
    or made of peanuts.

That could be a thing, I guess.
    Have I situated myself,
    or was I situated here by others,
    next to a stream, which brings a flow of minerals,

I'm not even aware of,
because it has so become part of me.

Were I to be replanted elsewhere,
away from such a source of life,
I would surely wither,
unless I contracted with an irrigation company,
which promised me a regular dose of the good stuff.

Yet where are the good, dependable streams and rivers these days?

2.8 THE REFUGE OF TREES: TWELVE FRUITS

winter

Coming to the end of my journey,
    I stop to stare at a tree by the river.
    I count twelve branches.

The January air hangs chilly around the twigs,
    yet I still see dried fruit hanging,
    and I feel my hunger, so I
    reach, grab, spit-shining
    till its wizened skin reflects the sun.

And I bite in.

Falling into a state of unknowing,
I awaken under the lit-up night sky,
and see Peter wrestling a man who carries water,
yet, this is the sort of energy, candour and wilfulness
one could expect from a Reubenite.

Then I arise and wander on for weeks,
having been nourished by this tree's bounty
for a time.

And prowling throughout the city,
despairing my workaday,
having forgotten of the refuge of trees,
those who nourish us,
suddenly I stop as I look up again
at that tree by the river.

Through a parting in the branches I see,
it's full of fruit, or are they nuts perhaps,
something different
than what I tasted a month ago.
I know my belly aches,
so I take a chance on this.

Now sensing a pain in my back,
I lift my head from the twisted root,
which I apparently called my pillow
for the last few hours,
and I find the heavens filled,
with James playing in the waves,
with a large fish,
a friendly whale of sorts.

This scene makes me think
of the reliability, the diligence
and preserving character of a Simeonite.
I splash my face with water from the river,
checking for whales.

The nuts are digesting,

bringing colour to my skin,
and I can tarry on again,
while days turn into weeks.

And now I'm back again at the river to pray,
where the canopy of this arboreal parent
greets me, seeing both my wonder and fatigue.

As I rest my head back on the trunk,
another dried fruit falls on my head,
and though startled,
my hand reflexes to snap it out of the air,
before it gets soiled on the ground.

With a glint in my eye,
I greedily sink my teeth into its overripe flesh.
The core, the seeds, I even chew the stem into a pulp,
and swallow down the mix of empowerment,
expecting in it a magical cure.

And now I look up through barely opened eyelids,
and there's a twinkling chorus conducted by a ram,
and there's the beloved John,
quick-witted, capricious and ever full of cheer,
the heroic tenor.
Ah, what a sanctimonious Levite!

But I quickly depart from this celestial symphony,
and let my feet amble onward,
to a destiny that a time and a half will let unfold.

In a fortnight or two my urban paths lead me,
again to this tree by the river,
having seen three of its branches bear such fruit,

I arrive expectant as the start of a new season unfolds.

I'm not disappointed.
In this springtime of my life,
as the boney limbs now bud with fresh sap,
blossoms have burst,
showering down their gorgeous vale
upon my head.

spring

My hair now covered,
I massage these perfumes into my scalp,
until the strands become matted,
and feel the tension dissipate
before the ecoscape that ensues.

The blanket of darkness descends,
and discloses the bull,
ridden by Andrew,
like such a western cowboy.
Yet I'm marvelling
at how considerately, imaginatively and sensitively
he appears to join this beast's movements,
while still bearing the marks of a warrior Judahite.

Dizzied with wonder at what these branches behold,
I'm beckoned by the invitation at the dawn
of new days and new ways.

My steps march back now,
with military might,
returning to the boughs
where I have found sanctuary these few months.

As the blossom pedals wax,
now wane and make way,
for a seed-like bud,
one that carries potency for flesh,
in the seasons to come.
Removing the last petals,
I snap the tiny core off the twig,
and dare to chew its sourness
as the unmet potential for growth
burns on my tongue.

And here,
the aftertaste still dancing on my palate,
my eyes glimpse the outline of twins,
playing monkey in the middle with Bartholomew.
I'm stunned as the game lasts for hours,
and I'm gripped in judgment
by the enthusiasm, the pride and the arrogance
of this Danielite.

Having wandered further on,
I wade barefoot through the stream,
and finding no place to rest for weeks,
I journey on with pruned feet,
until my toe is stubbed on the rock
that lies beneath the tree
with twelve branches,
and my seasons are now half-lived.

With nothing hanging from the limbs,
which my tongue hasn't yet known,
I look below to view its reflection
in the still waters below,
where a fallen limb has made for a quiet pool.

I spot a slug on the log,
feasting on fallen leaves,
and without a second's thought,
I pop it in my mouth,
as my sudden feverish hunger
reaches near delirium.

With soaking pants,
I awaken on the bank,
to peer up through twisted branches,
where a crab is tangled with the other Jacob,
and their entwined moves comport
a sort of elegance, even perfection despite their pickiness.

Is this coelestial crab
a reflection of the one snapping at my feet?
Ouch!
And this I ask,
knowing well this scene before me
could be performed by none other than a Naphtalite.

And half-lived but not half-baked,
my soul wanders forth
as my legs scramble to catch up,
now wending again to and fro,
and at last toward that enchanted arboreal sage,
the seat where I can peer out at my lode-star.

summer

In the growing heat,
my head and skin are longing for shade,
and as I trip over an exposed root,
and catch my fall

against the wall-like permanence of the trunk,
my hand crushes a termite,
which had hoped to find a dead branch to devour.

Having squashed it unbeknownst,
I crush it with my teeth,
before swallowing it down
with the sweat that is pouring off my brow.

And now the familiar scene,
my vision stirred by the sparkles in the sky,
Judas is trying to tame the Lion,
and though I know how this story ends,
I try to find him equitable, charming and I notice his hesitation,
while his mercenary qualities belie his Gadite heritage.

Feeling the relief of the cool night air,
forgetting the coming oppression of the noonday sun,
lost again for weeks
in the militancy of mortar blocks and jagged structures.

With a notion of short-sighted longevity,
the disorientation of impermanence
leads back to the sacred branches.

The blossoms and buds of those seemingly endless days,
of short weeks gone past,
have exposed an intention of fruit,
so tart, just a whiff wreaks their pungent power
like electricity through my tastebuds.

My stomach rumbles just at the thought,
but my appetite for such destruction,
overcomes my sense of order.

And the dream excites,
and my awareness perks,
and a virgin dances with Thaddeus,
as they tango, and become flung,
eyes closed, now open
and wild with desire.

Ah, the insight, mystery and suspicion
that surrounds this chaste courtship,
so typical of an Asherite.

In these days of summer's end,
my footsteps feeling fluid,
and my fitbit reads a million,
since I last slumped by that trunk;
on the horizon I gaze at that place of belonging.

As I near the branches,
the fruit hangs low.
And though it's large enough,
it smells of acid,
as the photosynthesizing
is still underway.

I stand with my hands
folded behind my back,
and like a child at Hallowe'en,
giggling in the effort to bite
at an apple hung with string,
I nip at the still tough skin,
until the juicy flesh is pierced.

Teeth tanging with the testimony of taste,
the atmosphere has beckoned me to audit,

to witness the scales balancing
in the cosmic delight of judgements,
while Matthew points from left to right,
noticing the inequality of reality,
feeling unconstrained, lively yet rash,
and he knows himself to be so scholarly,
such an Issacharite.

With days still sunny,
but nights getting cooler,
I amble back to the tree with twelve branches.

autumn

The weeks of my recent journey,
spent in the wonder and fervency of this season,
now chills as I watch the months fall.

The fruit now ripe,
or nearly so,
it crunches as I bite with confidence and candour.
This feels like the conclusion of a year,
yet I know all too well the labour
of this autumnal poise, posture and panic.

And the crisp air awakens the noetic nature,
as I watch Philip being stung by the scorpion,
which we knew lurked behind the clouds,
ready to attack in this season of fulfillment.
And though he remains perseverant, practical and solitary,
he does all the other Zebulunites proud.

My pace quickens now,
as the daytime cool air

puts muscles in motion,
generating some heat,
until I return to the expansive form,
nourishment for a soulful soil.

I touch the bark,
which encases a universe of fibres,
holding generations of renewal,
as the over-ripening of its produce,
can now be enjoyed with some caution.

The fallen fruit,
now full of worms it seems,
such soft pulp,
almost lurid sweetness.

And again, the half-fantastical moment arises,
as Simon, the stinking zealot he insists on being,
stands before the archer,
an apple propped on his head,
thinking he's so smart, liberal and ready for change,
but ready to suffer as a Josephite.

With but one month more to carry forth,
with the bending of the horizon toward winter,
hurried steps through wind-blown paths,
and leaves mixing about,
from so many a donation,
I arrive back at the twelve branches.

With the leaves now rid,
a new flora appears,
which had grown there all along.

Mystified at this oversight,
I cup a cluster of ripened grapes,
which just barely cling to their stems,
now cascading into a pile on my palm.

Greedily and half-mad,
with the knowledge that this harvest is now complete,
the oenophoric syrup runs down my chin.

I am drunk for days, perhaps,
my belly bulging with fullness,
not knowing when the Visitation will appear.

When at last an optical blur fades,
and a goat appears,
which Thomas is tending,
leading to a fro,
feeding it grass and watching it buck with delight.
How much more romantic, kind and sentimental
could this Benjamite be?

Having been lost for a goodly twelve months,
in which my only chance of orientation,
tree of solace in a concrete jungle,
I refuse to depart now,
and I circle it, tracing the twelve branches,
recalling the visions that taught me
the twelve fruits.

The leaves piled up underfoot,
curled and ready to crinkle when touched,
these I gather into a sack,
which I will guard as so much gold,
and I will prepare them to be stored away,
until they are boiled into tea,
and drank,
curatively.
For the healing of the nations.

2.9 SAUVAGES NOBLESSES

Let my mind be changed from human to beast;
let an eternity pass over me in this transition.

I have watched as the entire edifice of human achievement,
all which had branches, upward and outward,
like a beanstock, way up into the clouds,
and took shape over thousands of years,
being lopped off at the trunk,
preserving only the roots.

Every branch was broken,
tender tinder,
now awaiting a spark.

Much beauty turned to so much rubble.

I saw the greatest fall from their heights.
I saw that all were equal now.
Only now.

I saw that the beasts,
    whom we formerly-humans had cared for,
    were puzzled as to how they might be fed,
    and I watched as they turned on each other.
    It was ghastly. But exciting.

The birds no longer had a place to nest;
    not even the insects they loved,
    could find decaying fruit
    for nourishment.

I felt hunger,
    so I moved about with no aim,
    but to quell the pangs of my appetite,
    and felt at peace,
    after I filled my belly and could find rest.

Then I stood up,
    with the mind of a beast,
    no longer praising or bemoaning or grieving
    the fallen human edifice,
    no longer seeking to rebuild it,
    and discovered I had wandered back to the stump.

I placed a metal band of iron and bronze around it,
    laid down my head,
    waiting now for the dew from heaven
    to shower over me,
    knowing I've become equal with the beasts,

now sharing in their fierce innocence.

2.10 SIGNPOST - GROW FREE

Why did you leave me,
    alone, without strength to move on?
    Will you allow this anger to stay?
    Or will you be here with me?

It was you who shook the scaffold,
    all the while I constructed,
    and when I'd fallen,
    showed me the cracks in the fundament.
    If you can take it all apart,
    then I guess you're the one who'll rebuild.

You made me stare death in the face,
    and all I had left was cheap rye,
    to whet my tongue,
    and quench my thirst for what's real.

Is this here a signpost,
    pointing the way to

where you are parting the sea;
back to being the way
you want me to be?
Answer me here and now,
my patience has worn:
Are you showing me
how to grow free\

\to build on sand or on stone?/

As I said these words,
as nature and heaven heard,
The earth bowed its head to its source.
"Yeah I was delighted of course" says God,
that you're turning to me and
this is just what I'm about.

I'm ready for God's struggle.
I can sit down.
This fight is for God and not me.

Just point the way,
where resistance displays.
Lord are you ahead and with and behind us?
We need your compass,
because as humans, we're lost,
so let's lose ourselves in godness.

2.11 GET

I've found a place of rest
    in the comforts of home life,
    yet I'm so exhausted in this state.

I've lost my true bearing,
    even though there's a gentleness and peace around me.

But do I trust anyone to guide me?
    Can anyone tell me why I feel lost?

I've learned skills and bought equipment,
    and tools to keep me safe and secure.

When I face tough times again,
    will I find the energy to get up,
    get busy,
    get moving,
    get going,
    get doing...

My cup is half full and yes,
also half empty;
I do realize reality has two sides,
and wisdom has two faces.

My wife bought me my favourite cologne,
so many years ago.
And it's only half used,
so, yeah,
I'm good for now.

I have walked away from the house of the Lord,
and at times my walk was a run.
And I do think I know my way back.
Maybe.
Probably.

2.12 Asherah Beside the Altar

When I was told,
we shall build an altar to the Lord,
I rejoiced.

My mind started spinning with ideas,
mental blueprints of a structure,
impossible beams,
dynamic angles and trusses
in constant motion,
so complex was their design,
beholding emotions,
expressions to the Almighty.

But it needed to be solid,
bold and broad,
natural-looking yet finely hand-crafted.

We needed it to be a portal to the divine.

And that's why we needed to have beside it,
a symbol of our connection to the divine,
in the shape of a tree.

There was no question.
There was no hesitation.
It all fit together so well.

As we would approach the altar,
as the focal point of our sacramental commu-
nication,
we would be greeted by Asherah,
the wooden portent overseeing the encounter,
like a mothering sentinel,
radiant in beauty,
humbly planted in the earth,
yet stretching in every direction,
like an explosion of life,
that would not be contained by space and time.

But now,
what is this you're saying?
"Don't plant an Asherah,
beside the altar to the Lord?"
Is this simple jealousy,
or just another attempt to confuse me
about the relationship between
the flora and the sacred?

2.13 PINING FOR REFUGE IN ROME

Signore, tu m'hai saggiato e mi conosci

As the great Horticulturalist, you looked me over and
understood me fully

Tu sai quando mi siedo e mi levo

You know the seasons of my growth, repose and decline

tu comprendi da lungi il mio pensiero

You keep watch over me from a distance and you know how I
express myself with soothing aromatics and anti-bacterial
phytoncides

quando cammino e quando riposo, tu mi scruti

You get how I need to stretch out adroitly and also to rest
sometimes, and just droop

e a fondo, tutte le mie vie ti son note

It seems you know me to the core

Ché la parola non è ancora sulla mia bocca,

Even before I'm ready to sprout a bud, which will turn into a new basket of seeds

ed ecco, che tu, Signore, già la conosci tutto

You're also such a great Botanist, you already know it's going to happen!

Circondimi, stai di fronte e alle spalle

Somehow it feels like you are supporting me from all sides, from in *front and behind, simultaneously*

e poni la tua mano su di me

while your loving hands are gently fanning my tender needles

La scienza che hai di me è meravigliosa

How on earth do you do all that? This puzzles me down through the ends of my messy roots

è sublime; troppo alta perché io possa arrivarci

and sometimes I'm not sure whether to feel assured or creeped out!

Dove me n'andro lontano dal tuo Spirito

Because if I wanted to escape this care you give me, your *cultura hortensi,* to become carelessly independent and wildly free

e dove fuggirò dalla tua faccia-presenza?

what corner of the biosphere would allow me to subsist apart from you?

Se salirò in cielo tu ci sei

If my branches reach directly upward, I enter your space of dwelling

se scenderò nel soggiorno dei morti, eccoti là

If my roots dig down, into the realm of all that is decaying, you're also present there!

Se prendo le ali sul mattino

If a gentle bird lands on me, and the wind allows my needle clusters to follow her in flight

e abitare all'estremità del mare

or if a part of me snaps off in a windstorm and floats upon the sea, and then plunges to its depths

anche colà mi condurrà la tua mano

your green thumb leads the way to the shore

e mi terrà stretto la tua destra

even as you grip me firmly

Se dico: «Certo le tenebre mi occulteranno

And although I might speak the words, "I smell smoke, and I bet I will soon become smothered in a thick blanket of ashes"

e pur la luce diventerà notte intorno a me»,

your light will shine through the opacity

Perch è le tenebre stesse non possono nasconderti nulla

so that it will seem like I'm in full sun

e la notte per te splenderà come il giorno

It seems there is no difference for you, whether it's night or day

cosi le tenebre e la luce ti sono uguali

Light and dark are the somehow indifferent for you

Sei tu che possiedi le mie reni

You engineered my DNA

che m'hai preso ed intessuto nel seno di mia madre.

Creating me first as a seed, with all the healthy growth potential I have in this life

Io ti celebro, perché sono stato fatto in modo stupendo.

And I've become your biggest fan, waving at you with the
breadth of my twigs and needles, shivering with delight

Mirabili sono le tue opere,

I'm amazed at all you can do – such creativity!

e l'anima mia ben lo sa

All my inner rings, from my bark to my core, are aware of this

La mia ossatura non ti erano nascoste,

You were fully in tune with the shape I would become and my
purpose for growth here, this soil where I'm rooted

quando fui formato nel segreto

and you knew this already when I was but a tiny seed that fell
loose from a pine cone

e la mia sostanza nelle profondità della terra

And somehow I found the right depth in the soil to boldly
sprout upward and anchor myself with a fragile root

la massa informe del mio corpo, i tuoi occhi videro

and already then, you could somehow perceive the fuller vista,
the forest surrounding the tree I'd become

e eran tutti scritti nel tuo libro

and in your botanist textbook, your great Almanac, all these things were written

i giorni che mi sto destinando

detailing each mm of my gradual aching and pining for existence

quando nessuno d'essi, sorto era ancora

and that was before I even gained traction in the soil

Oh, Dio! quanto mi sono preziosi i tuoi pensieri

I'm enthralled with the very idea of your *cultura hortensi*

Quant'è grandissime il loro insieme!

and I feel like such a stump, when I even try to guess how much you might know!

Se li voglio contare, sono più numerosi che minuscoli ciottoli

I can't even count my needles, but I bet that number is pretty small in comparison to the number you've tallied

e mi levo e sono ancora con te

I can sense your presence, even when my thoughts are at rest

Oh! Certo, tu sterminassi l'empio, o Dio

There are so many bugs and fungi, which threaten me, and I know you can exterminate them all *perciò allontanatevi da me questi uomini sanguinari*

But I still feel like screaming, "bug off, you dreadful swarm!

Essi parlano contro di te sadicamente

And yes, I *can* hear you mocking the great Hortaculturist!"

i tuoi nemici si servono del tua nomina per sostenere la menzogna

I even saw them use your Almanac when they were buzzing around, with a sarcastic meme about *cultura hortensi*

Signore, non odierò forse quelli che ti odiano?

So why would I not hope for the demise of those who give you grief?

E non detesterò quelli che insorgono contro di te?

How can I hesitate to spew my phytoncides in all directions, exploding with my alpha-pinene, careen, myrcene, and other terpenes?

Io li odierò di un odio perfettissimo

I feel rooted in the goal of their extermination

miei nemici, son essi per me

and I wager my existence on this

Saggiami, o Dio, e conosci il mio cuore

Run your lab tests on my bark and my branches, every last mm of *the space I consume in this forest*

Mettimi alla prova e conosci le mie viei

Consider what is bugging me, and see what a futile mess this is

E vedi se c'è in me qualche via iniqua, del male

Please determine if my DNA is corrupted, and figure out if I'm to be coated in fungicide

e guidami per la strada eterna

And let me stay firmly planted as long as there is Co2 for me to clean, and a need for more oxygen in the forest!

2.14 137 RELOADED

Alongside the developments with strip malls and box stores,
with over- and under-passes,
we sat in the ditch and we cried,
recalling when nature had been wild and free.

We placed our smart phones on the benches
at the bus shelter,
and saw passers-by who flocked
for the latest deals, the greatest of upgrades.

They saw us sitting in the ditch,
playing with blades of grass,
and tapping sticks against each other,
and we heard,
"what's wrong? Forget to upgrade your Spotify account?
Can't find any tracks that glorify the wilderness-ditch you're in?"

But how can we sit,
facing such a mammoth development,
which mocks nature,
and enjoy a song that glorifies the gods of this destruction?

If we ever lose sight of the vision of tangled trees,
and soggy swamps
and rivers that wind their own paths,
then I hope at least I will never sell out,
never give up saying
that we can't back down from what is good and true;
we can't build a world by taming the wild,
and we need to teach kids,
the wild *is* our home.

Remember the capitalists and communists,
whose persistent economics put our wild to ruin,
when development tried to tame us all,
through words and roads and tools and and and,
the developers of strip malls and box stores,
who seek profit from taming the wild.

They've tried to steal the Wild,
and scavenge the wilderness,
and whoever can get it back,
we will sing a song when liquidators come to town
and the weeds and shrubs
and bugs and slugs
take the whole! damned! place! back!

2.15 BUDDHA'S BEAU BO

The Buddha's Bodhi,
the beau Bo
at Bodh Gaya,
in the Bihar,
ficus religiosa:
a pipal of the people,
for Gautama,
circa 500 BCE,
to become the Bhagavathi,
Bull among men,
the Dharmaraja,
Lord of the Dhamma,
but boor among the Brahmans.

2.16 THE TAO OF TREES: AN AEROBIC SCRIPT

Push up

pull down

now spread

and criss-cross

while anchored

still moving

now drink

and tan

now fast

yet still

now resting

yet bursting

and now and yet and how!

Once more, here we go,

push up

pull down

....

A KNOWLEDGE MEANT

Speaking of reverence in playfulness, for those who thought I was a serious scholar of divine mathematics, don't worry. I still could be, maybe. And though I do bemoan those who can't have fun whilst they pontificate on these matters, I won't write a further disclaimer about hoping not to have offended anyone by going for the jocular at times (and perhaps it's already too late), because if anyone is afraid to raise a defiant fist and shake it at the Almighty as the Psalmist also does at times, I wonder if they are taking the matter of coelestial wondering seriously enough. And in raising a fist, it can be helpful to be coy or nakedly ridiculous, and search for that ephemeral moment that suggests fissures are appearing in the traces of a border between the humorous and the tragic as we decay into an untold oblivion. Of this I've learned as much from the comedics of my extended Mennonite family as from pagan spirituality of the ancient Greeks. Shakespeare, on the other hand, was surely a poser in comparison. But Maria Bamford beats them all.

Heretofore, I owe as much to Richard Wagamese as to Leonard Cohen, Robert Service, Al Purdy, Dylan Thomas and his Jewish-Minnesotan namesake, the erstwhile Robert Zimmerman, Friedrich Nietzsche and Tom Waits. Carlton Douglas Ridenhour probably taught me more about the near-mystical fighting power of the performative word than all the aforementioned white folks combined. Yes, "As the rhythm's designed to bounce, what counts is that the rhyme's designed to fill your mind." So very true. What else does a student of poetry need to learn? And with Ridenhour, I give myself permission to let obscure references and quips and quirks lie in the text, which function as icons to a folder that resides in the cloud storage of my dusty mental shelves, for a curious reader to click on, investigate, and puzzle over upon realizing my operating system isn't fully upgraded; or preferably, simply allow them to float past and notice their aesthetic wick-wicky-wack. I should also acknowledge how influential Qoheleth has been for me, along with Grimmelhausen's *Simplicius Simplicissicimus* and there should be no shame in my adding Alfred E. Neuman to this list of venerable *literati*. This list is obviously getting too long, so it must end before it becomes a bibliography of every book I've ever read.

Please do forgive the classical language flourishes, which creep in on occasion. They're not meant to impress or intimidate. They are not, as some might assume, a residue of my training at the Pontifical Institute of Mediaeval Studies, rather, the inspiration for my careening Latin insertions derives from my renewed fascination with Ernest P. Worrell's habit of faux-Latin quips. Ergo, Mary, in these classical linguistic hiccups I might be heard as taking on a similarly mocking tone, meant for fun, not confusion. Y'know what I mean, Vern? Please accept or ignore them as one of my mirthful misfires. In gratitude I would also blame Bliss Carmen for this linguistic discretion, whose classic poem, the title and structure and theology of which I've pilfered and distorted and perhaps even vilified, is unfortunately treated as equal to Scripture on some innocent soils, and deserves at least some teasing if we are to take its ideas seriously. If anyone were to suggest all these loose verbal parts and loosened poetics here presented are but bumbling attempts to de-throne that ex-poet laureate, I may struggle to contradict that assertion.

I would equally admit my guilt of a similar intent to chide

in my homage to J.J. Rousseau, who was my first love in the field of sincere humanist philosophy. I will spare him my scolding for his horrid contributions in the field of gender relations, as I glare adoringly at that Swiss genius, now from a distance of almost three centuries, in our state somewhere between enlightenment and vexation.

Although I am claiming copyright to this whole collection, I suppose my son Simeon could contend that he co-authored "Norm's Song" but since I was the one who held the pen, he has no legal proof of his contribution.

LONG AFTERWARD

SELF-DEFEATING CAVEATS, SELF-CONGRATULATORY EXCUSES, SELF-AGGRANDIZING INNUENDOS, SELF-DESTRUCTIVE EXPLANATIONS AND SELF-LOATHING GENEALOGIES

Please don't read this as an explanatory afterword. Or at all. Unless you feel you must. I will sleep better knowing that you've read this book without needing to dig into these next pages.

But if you're like me and need some blah-blah-blah by means of explanation afterward, be my guest. I didn't want to disappoint or give the impression my haste to publish was accompanied by laziness!

Welcome to my congregation of stray thoughts, at least those I managed to capture, scattered as they were on my desk and spread across the windshield of my life for a few years, getting to the point that it became hard find my laptop or to see the road ahead. It seemed too painful to consign them to the paper scrapper, before sharing a few of them with some friends. And let's not forget potential future frenemies, of course.

This book took shape near the end of a particularly challenging and unrelated writing project, which, though very stimulating and enjoyable, left me needing some sort of outlet for my thoughts, something akin to the NHL player who feels the urge to do pirouettes as a break from his power-skating drills. As the forest bathing practice I work on with Melissa (nnft.ca) has deepened my desire and ability to connect with nature, and with the further stimulus of the certification course I've been taking with the *Child & Nature Alliance of Canada* (CNAC), I realized my thoughts can untangle most easily when directed toward the world of trees. And I've discovered this isn't new for me, it's just new that I'm making a practice of it. In fact, I found out some of these poems go back a few years, including "Please Please Please, Stop" which was a high-school geography project.

I can't unpack where they all came from, or how they hang together as a whole. That's your job, or no one's, but it's not mine, though in prefatory excitement I may be tempted to try guide the reader, imagining I'm some sort of Virgil and you are my Dante as we plunge into the verbal inferno and purgatory that is my creativity. In this case, don't trust my conjectures masquerading as intellectual autobiographical blathering. I can't pretend this collection will make sense to many people; as someone who toils in rational word-smithing as a day-job, these sometime irrational, blithesome mutterings and textual splatterings called poetic verse frankly feel a little embarrassing and now sharing them leaves me exposed in a way that is both uncomfortable for me and awkward for the cautious and thus far unsuspecting reader.

While my professional labours involve making plain what is potentially hidden or obscure, a task in which creativity is often scorned, to deign the poetic practice has often served me as a release valve, sometimes resulting in a gaseous cloud of ostentatious confusion, that is, for anyone who needs words to be made plain to the point of dull. When poetry rids itself of such pedantic plainness, it more fully excites the imagination; the more words seem to make plain sense, the less interesting I find them, and therefore, I do feel several pieces in this collection are simply boring, in their explicability.

I once won a Remembrance Day poem contest in grade school, apparently before the local Legion committee knew better than to decorate a Mennonite kid with such military honour. I hold the participating Legion members at least partly responsible for instilling the requisite confidence, which would blossom almost four decades later into this book. But no, I'm not that interested in buying the poppies you want to sell me.

That debutante's poem was, "Wars Should Never Have Started" and although I have most of it still tucked away in the recesses of the grey matter, I don't have a full copy of it, nor would I have wanted to include it here, as it makes me shutter with embarrassment from its sincere naiveté. Yet, if pushed, I would insist that the world needs a whole lot more simplicity than it enjoys, especially in the printed word; yet I'm admittedly too shy to be a *bona fide* purveyor or peddler of such. Let's leave that to the populist political pundits, shall we? I'm always eager to welcome the sheep in our midst who are dressed in wolves' clothing, without wanting to out them. More on that in a forthcoming publication, pending review by the Gelassenheit editorial board. Fingers crossed.

In addition to the Legion's *laudatio*, I could mention that I have been given the odd nudge and pat on the head by a few others, leading me to believe that my writings, which derive from a psychic space beneath the blurred vision that sometimes impairs my usual labour, might in fact have some place in civil society, despite their initial purpose being nothing than to suit my own personal fancy. I'm grateful for the feedback I've received on occasions when I've dared to share.

I do admit however, that my Remembrance Day poem planted the seed in my child-like mind, part hope and part hubris, that I do have poems rattling around my noggin at times, like so many loose screws, which need to be put on paper in order to stop them from disturbing my usual steely focus. Rarely are they shared with anyone, except my gracious wife, Melissa, who understands both my coy sincerity and my irreverent naiveté. At least I think she does. She may disconfirm that, and disavow me of that assumption after reading this collection which I am dedicating to her, as the love of my life. So much loving through twenty years of marriage, and still counting on so many more to come.

Melissa and I share a deep love of trees and the natural world, and this fast became an enduring bond that rooted our friendship as we began dating in NYC, grafting our lives together over two decades ago, whilst trying as often as possible to escape the grasp of that city, either in the bosom of Central Park, or via the Metro-North railway into the Hudson Valley. We also shared a need to wrestle with concepts of the divine as presented in nature. It's been a long journey that I know so many of us are on, and I hope it never ends or gets too sanctimonious. This collection is an unscientific report of my investigations thus far on *natura naturata*. Although I've let the odd reference to *natura naturans* slip in if only *sotto voce*, for a fuller account of how Spinoza's panentheism is relevant to our daily lives, I would refer interested readers to my dissertation, *From Antinomy to Sophiology* (2008).

The title poem expresses the grafting of loyalties I've felt to trees and to people seeking refuge, perhaps most notably my own need to escape the mortar. My rendition of this escapade is a biblically-infused thought experiment accompanied by the zodiac, involving casual, cosmic intersectionalities. I have more often found refuge under or in a tree, than in the houses of the holy, although if pressed I'll admit that since such houses are typically made of wood to some degree, in like measure they too can provide some refuge. Through a career involving years of treeplanting, nature-connection and youth programming, and more recently forest therapy guiding, various forms of refugee sponsorship have also played a major role in phases of my work and life experience in finding my place in this world, relating with the other two-legged, non-forest creatures who need to operate within the violent geopolitical lines we so love to impose upon two-dimensional maps and then affix to our noses as though aptly-fractured lenses, through which to view the decline of the Anthropocene.

Having been a historical and linguistic translator and editor, a part of me is bursting to unpack the meanings of many of my poems in pedantic paragraphs, trying to justify how they make sense to me. But that would be to proffer a lie. They won't always make sense, and I know that when I read a poem whose background story torments my curiosity, I'm probably better off not knowing its origins or having a hermeneutical crutch handed to me by its author. That would surely ruin the fun that our imaginations afford us.

And now permit me to feign a reversal of what I just wrote about my reticence concerning the background of these writings by explaining the organizational structure herein. The dividing line between the two categories is whether or not I can identify or admit to any significant connection of what I've written to the traditional canon of Hebrew or Christian Scripture, although I've also tucked in a couple deriving from eastern spiritual sources, among the Judeo-Christian. The first section, therefore, I've called "Pseudo-Spiritual" since I would rather tell you that these writings are *not* authentically spiritual and be contradicted, than vice versa. And I won't insult anyone's intelligence by further explaining the nature of the second section, except to list as many verses as I can, in no particular order, which, I would insist, gave me licence to unpack the stanzas of this section. Further, as to avoid the appearance that one ought to look up the biblical passages that lurk behind all the poems in this section, I'm erecting a hurdle in the path, a stumbling stone, by providing the book:chapter reference only in the original language, the Hebrew and Greek original.

2.1-2, 320 ,2.6 ;יִרְמְיָהוּ 6 ,2.5 ;מִשְׁלֵי 8 ,2.4 ;אִיּוֹב 12 ,2.3 ;מִשְׁלֵי
2.8 ;יִרְמְיָהוּ 17 ,2.7 ;דְּבָרִים Η Αποκάλυψη του Ιωάννη 22; 2.9,
4 139 ,2.13 ;דְּבָרִים 16 ,2.12 ;מִשְׁלֵי 23 ,2.11 ;מִשְׁלֵי 60 ,2.10 ;דָּנִיֵּאל
מִשְׁלֵי 137 ,2.14 ;מִשְׁלֵי

No biblical translations were intentionally harmed in the making of these poems, with the possible exception of "Pining for Refuge in Rome" in which a combination of my *speranza* and Esperanto may have hijacked my best of intentions to produce an original translation in Italian.

Several of the poems in both sections have also taken on a life as songs, although if I'm honest, not all have passed the "Beatles test" as their tunes either abruptly or more gradually faded from my memory, and I haven't yet run across any bootlegged recordings of them. A couple of them I've sung and played for others and could still reproduce in some tonal fashion if the occasion presented itself. For those, which will never be resurrected as melodies, may they hereby rest in peace as mere words until someone else tries to whistle them forthwith.

"Is it too late to withdraw this project from the public's eye?" I ask out loud for absolutely no one to hear. In reply, again for no one to hear, another voice asks, "Is this guy trying to be funny?" I can but hint or intimate: indeed, these pages are quite potentially a vain attempt to disguise the discomfort, embarrassment and malaise of being overly serious. And caring too deeply. And now I hear someone else ask, “Is this just a bunch of nature Romantism?” The reply: “Um, I don’t think so,” mumbles the hapless, barefoot Romantic.

Many thanks to the good folks at Gelassenheit Publications, who yielded to my request to hurry up the final proofs on this volume to beat the Christmas rush.

Finally, my gratitude to Fraser Lake Camp, meaning the people and place it has been for me and others. Here's hoping that camp and others like it will remain viable spaces to discover purpose in life for us ambling peons for poetic aeons to come.

Jonathan Seiling
St Catharines, Ontario, December 2020

About the Author

As a mortar-person, Jonathan Seiling is often occupied with editing and translating early modern religious radicalism, while he daydreams about the twilight of the Anthropocene. From time to time he also likes to take a break from all sorts of projects involving actual mortar to get lost in the woods where he can practice relating to people better by talking to the trees.

www.ingramcontent.com/pod-product-compliance
Lightning Source LLC
Chambersburg PA
CBHW051953290426
44110CB00015B/2226
9780988099319